SkyBiz 2000 is unlike ANY OTHER home-based business—EVER! It is NEW, UNIQUE, INNOVATIVE, COSTS $110 TOTAL to TRY, and it is making MILLIONAIRES faster and easier than any other business in history, home-based or otherwise. Interested?

PLEASE, don't be afraid to TRY. You can start this PART-TIME and it WILL excite you because it could change your life and lifestyle (and those of your children) FOREVER!

This book is written for those who have dreams of being rich. You simply *cannot* do it by working for someone else—you have to be in business for yourself. But how do you do it?

You have a family so you can't go back to school. You have little or no money so you can't make a loan to start a business. You don't have a college degree. You have no special skills. You've worked for someone else in some menial JOB most of your life. What CAN you do? This book has the answers.

If you TRULY want to become RICH by working for yourself, read the entire book. It tells you the truth—how you can make it, how you can fail, why you might have failed in the past and how to do it the right way *this* time.

BECOME AN

Internet Millionaire

Featuring

SKYBIZ 2000

How to Succeed in a Home-Based Business

EARN $1,000,000 a Year

by

PETE BILLAC

Swan Publishing

Author: Pete Billac
Editors: Kerry Dancy, Dave Zaruca, Stuart Purcell,
Dr. Margaret Yates, and Chuck Galvin, D.V.M.
Layout Artist: Kimberly Newell, Sharon Davis
Cover Design: John Gilmore

OTHER BOOKS BY PETE BILLAC:

The Annihilator
The Last Medal of Honor
How Not to be Lonely—TONIGHT
All About Cruises
New Father's Baby Guide
Willie the Wisp
Lose Fat While You Sleep
Managing Stress
The Silent Killer

Swan Publishing
Library of Congress Catalog Card #00-101730
ISBN# 0-943629-45-4

BECOME AN INTERNET MILLIONAIRE is available in quantity discounts through Swan Publishing, 126 Live Oak, Alvin, TX 77511. Phone: (281) 388-2547, Fax: (281) 585-3738, or e-mail: swanbooks@ghg.net. Website: http://www.swan-pub.com

Printed in the United States of America.

In most books, this is the DEDICATION PAGE. I wanted to use it to explain my *style* of writing. I write in BIG print, SMALL words, I RESEARCH my topics thoroughly, and I go RIGHT AT THE JUGULAR. My words are CAPITALIZED, *italicized*, **bold faced** and with "quotation marks." Since most of my books are in the *How-To* category, I want to make ABSOLUTELY certain that there is **no room** for even a *hint* of MISINTERPRETATION. Let me explain.

As a kid in grade school, teachers said I had a fantastic memory; not smart, just—a good MEMORY. I *remember* a six-line example of how a single word—EMPHASIZED—changes the meaning of the entire sentence: I NEVER SAID HE STOLE THAT!

I never said he stole that!
I **NEVER** said he stole that!
I never **SAID** he stole that!
I never said **HE** stole that!
I never said he **STOLE** that!
I never said he stole **THAT**!

And THAT, my critics, professional writers, and English teachers is **why** I chose to put the *emphasis* on certain words. Just blame it on *my* "writing style." I dedicate this book to you.

Forget the rules. Find a good story, use BIG print, tell it in "plain" words people can understand, offer only the truth, don't make the book too long, and go write your own best seller.

FOREWORD

If you TRULY want to become RICH—an INTERNET MILLIONAIRE—this book will give you the BEST chance at becoming wealthy beyond your wildest dreams!

The *computer age* is upon us. Most successful BIG businesses use the computer as their primary tool. Most home-based businesses, Internet or not, use the computer to help run whatever business they are attempting to do at home.

I highlight ***SkyBiz 2000*** because **IT GOT ME EXCITED!** It is a business you can work at home using your computer and your telephone, and earn MORE money, FASTER and EASIER, than ANY home-based business in history.

THINK ABOUT IT! There is NO product to buy, lug around or store in your garage. There are NO monthly quotas. It costs $110 TOTAL to start. It is FAST, EASY, and SOME are making $25,000+ a WEEK in LESS THAN A YEAR since joining!

Just about ANYONE can do it. You don't need a college degree, you don't have to have prior training, and you don't have to invest more than the price of a cheap suit to TRY. You can even STAY with your present job, just give yourself a CHANCE to make more—you'll NEVER get rich with a JOB!

I'm reaching out ONLY to those who truly WANT to be rich. Oh, this book tells how to be successful in any, and ALL, home-based businesses! And, I understand that "rich" means different things to different people, but I refuse to get involved with, *"Rich is how many friends you have,"* or "*Rich is when you are in love,"* etc., etc. I'm talking about only MONEY rich!

I mean those who want to own a home that costs $500,000 **UP**. I'm talking about you AND your spouse driving a new car EVERY year! I mean going on exotic vacations or cruises whenever you want and really enjoying being RICH!

MONEY has but ONE sense; *hearing.* Tell it what to do and it does it. Tell it right and you win. Tell in wrong and you lose. CALL it loudly enough and it'll come to you. **SkyBiz 2000 SHOUTED at people!** Their voice was heard AROUND THE WORLD!

SkyBiz 2000 is in over 130 COUNTRIES, and with the **punch of a button,** it translates the information, currently, into 15 foreign languages. Can YOU see how **powerful** this is? Can you understand how much MONEY is being made by those who began with one-hundred and ten dollars TOTAL investment?

SOME who WERE "aware" of the power of the Internet JOINED **SkyBiz 2000** and went directly to work, are earning (in less than one year) $5,000, $10,000 and $25,000 a **WEEK**!

The TOP guy (companies always like to mention those, and rightfully so) who has been in this phenomenal company for a bit over a year, is earning over $125,000 a WEEK and will probably be up to a million dollars a MONTH in the next eight to ten months.

I do NOT work for **SkyBiz 2000**. I'm not being paid by them, nor have they invested in my book. This is all on my own. Whatever I write or intimate is MY OWN DOING. I sell books. The INTERNET, **SkyBiz 2000,** and making MILLIONS is synonymous!

If YOU want to become an INTERNET MILLIONAIRE, read more of this book. If you want only to make a few hundred thousand dollars a year in ANY home-based business, PLEASE read this book.

SkyBiz 2000 is making MILLIONAIRES over the Internet. Find out HOW. It is EASY to do, inexpensive to TRY, and if you want to put in the time, use your BRAIN and become RICH, it's yours for the taking.

You can NEVER get rich at a JOB! You are WORKING to *exist*; the **boss** has the best chance at becoming rich. So, YOU be the boss! YOU hire hundreds—THOUSANDS of employees, all people working for you, and you pay them NOTHING!

Yes, **SkyBiz 2000** is making new millionaires as the clock ticks. I include TRUE stories in this book from which you can identify. **I GET EXCITED** as I interview these people, when I SEE THEIR CHECKS, when I KNOW how much they're making. It is hard to believe; **I** didn't believe it! But, it's all TRUE!

I hope **YOU GET EXCITED**! Get that adrenaline flowing. Use you HEAD and find out more. This COULD be YOUR chance to change your life and lifestyle FOREVER! Too many others have done it, ARE doing it—"regular" people just like you and me.

I wrote a book about 14 years ago that grossed more than 48 million dollars! No publisher would take it; they said I had **"NO RELEVANT CREDENTIALS"** to write such a book, so I started my own home-based business, published the book myself, and got rich.

NOW, I want to help others realize their dreams. It's not the money with me anymore. It's *the game.* If YOU follow what I have to say and if you REALLY want to be rich, read this book.

Pete Billac

TABLE OF CONTENTS

Chapter 1

YOUR HOME-BASED BUSINESS

I, personally, do not work for nor do I represent ANY of these companies, but I researched them. I've interviewed several hundred distributors from various companies, and I'm here to tell you how to go about it. All of my how-to books are in sort of *story form* so you won't feel as though you're reading a text book. And, I'm candid!

If you are already IN a home-based business chances are, it IS *connected* to a Network Marketing company—the most popular source for those who are in a home-based business.

Do NOT be frightened by that word, *Network Marketing*, because one of the EASIEST ways to get rich (on your own) **is** to NETWORK! If you are already involved in a Network Marketing company, don't be ashamed of it, be PROUD!

And whether you are working part-time or full time, you are TRYING to become financially independent. If you make it, TERRIFIC. And if you FAIL, try again. "*If you don't TAKE a chance, you never HAVE a chance.*"

I "*bring to the table*" more than **four decades** of

study and research in home-based businesses. I KNOW why people have failed in the past and how I can guide them to "*making it work for them*" in the future. I wrote this book SOLELY for those who want to change their lifestyle and become RICH!

I can't guarantee it will happen to *everyone*, because each individual is different. But this book will guide you along the right path. It FEATURES **SkyBiz 2000**, but it tells about OTHER methods that work in ALL home-based businesses.

The amount of MONEY that *can be* made—that **is** *being* made by many in **SkyBiz 2000**—is **UNBE-LIEVABLE!** I can recall that only a decade or more ago, if a person was promised they could make $10,000 a *month*, every governmental agency in existence would "jump on them" with both feet.

NOW, people are making that much a **DAY** with **SkyBiz 2000** and the cost to TRY is only $110. There is **NO** product to carry in your car or store in your garage. There is **NO** monthly fee or quota. There are **NO MEETINGS** to attend, and it is a WAY for just about **ANYONE** who is *non*-rich, to BECOME rich!

When I found out that I *knew* several people IN **SkyBiz 2000** who had been unsuccessful in other Network Marketing companies and making a "killing" in this one, I went to them for their secrets. I became **SO EXCITED** that I had to share it with others.

One friend of mine who is now in **SkyBiz 2000,** is earning well OVER **$100,000 a MONTH** and he has been working at it **LESS THAN A YEAR!** His life has changed totally. I spoke with him a few days ago and he was on an all-time *high;* he was ecstatic.

"*Know what I did last week, Pete*?" he said with a self-satisfied tone. "*For years I had seen movies where the rich guy went into a bar and yelled, DRINKS ARE ON THE HOUSE! I always wondered how it would feel to be able to do that. Well,*" he continued, "*I DID IT! It wasn't a small bar either; there must have been 70 or 80 people drinking. And—IT FELT GREAT!*

"*People came up and thanked me, women (he's single) came up and offered to buy me a drink, a few asked me to dance, people patted me on the back, shook my hand. What a terrific feeling," he* went on. "It *was a silly fantasy, but IT CAME TRUE*!"

IN THIS BOOK, I *talk* to you as I would talk to a friend. Again, I write in BIG print, SMALL words most can read without a dictionary, and you needn't be college educated to read and understand it. I'm CANDID and TRUTHFUL.

And, you needn't be SMART to make this kind of MONEY. ANYONE can do it! Be willing to put in the time, take a chance, dream big, and TRY.

Network Marketing has produced MORE MILLIONAIRES than any other single industry in the world, INCLUDING the movie business and the sports world! However, BAD NEWS always takes the spotlight and OF COURSE people failed in Network Marketing.

MOST Network Marketing companies go out of business the first year! But then, **MOST NEW BUSI-**

NESSES of *all* types go out of businesses the FIRST YEAR!

I never want to insult you. But, I will TELL YOU THE TRUTH because that's the only way to be fair with you. I'm telling you ahead of time so you won't want to "punch me out" if we meet. If YOU failed in the past in networking, it's BECAUSE . . .

1. You didn't *research* the company or the pay plan; *STUPID*.

2. You *thought* you would make a MILLION DOLLARS with *little effort*. GREEDY *(and a little bit stupid, too*).

3. You were LAZY. You didn't TRY! You didn't REALLY work! You believed that "silk suit" in front of the room who said "Work PART-TIME 2 or 3 three hours a week and you can sail off on your yacht to Tahiti." *Naive, bordering on stupid.*

When will people understand that "THERE **IS** NO FREE LUNCH?" It's WORK to become rich! It is NOT easy. If it was, EVERYBODY would be rich. And "part time" is NOT a FEW hours a week. There's 168 hours in the week. MOST "regular" jobs take 60 or so hours working and driving to and from work. This leaves 108 HOURS (another 50 or so hours to sleep), and there are SIXTY-EIGHT **more** hours to spare.

Want to change your lifestyle and that of your

family? *Forever*? THEN GO INTO BUSINESS FOR YOURSELF! Read the FACTS on Network Marketing as a home-based business. It's a great CHANCE to change your financial life for the better.

If you presently ARE in Network Marketing, you can identify with much of this. Read it ALL, *please.* You might learn more and maybe get an idea or two that could make you successful. And if you're NOT in any and never been because you are wary of them, *hold on to your hat and get ready for a wild ride!*

NETWORK MARKETING

Below are some of the thoughts from those who know *little* about Network Marketing. MOST of these folks are ***working for somebody else*** and helping make THEM rich. MOST of them HEAR the *bad stuff* and have never TRIED. These people will NEVER know what it is to be RICH.

I'm not "knocking" them. We need all kinds in the world. They might be fine people, well regarded in their respective neighborhood, many are in or running some *homeowner's group*, they're heads of their entire block. In other words, they are—BLOCK HEADS.

What I'd like YOU to do (If you want to TRY to be rich) is smile, wave at them, be cordial, but by all means ABSENT YOURSELF from negative-thinking people. Do NOT let their comments or thoughts discourage YOU from pursuing your goal— becoming WEALTHY! Remember the phrase? "*If you think you*

CAN—or think you CAN'T—you're absolutely RIGHT!"

THESE PEOPLE WILL NEVER BE RICH!

Oh, I know, this will never work. I've tried it. (They've NEVER tried it; they aren't the type.)

This is another of those PYRAMID schemes. (This is when they REALLY don't know what they're talking about.)

I know too many who have failed at it. (Maybe so, maybe not. Many should NOT be in business for themselves.)

I don't want to have to visit someone's house and bother them. (There are MANY companies that *do not require* house visits.)

Nine out of TEN go out of business in less than a year. (So do MOST new businesses.)

If I have ONE MORE poor person trying to make ME rich, I'll punch them out. (Stay POOR then.)

I've tried it THREE times and each time it COST me money. (Greedy, lazy or stupid.)

I HATE meetings and I can never get anyone to go to a meeting with me. (Meetings are NOT NECES-

SARY in **SkyBiz 2000.**)

I've run out of friends, relatives and neighbors to talk to. (MY way creates a NEW warm market.)

NOBODY makes the kind of money you're talking about. (Right! Stay naive and unknowing.)

Only the ones who get in FIRST make the big money. (WRONG AGAIN!)

I am NOT a salesperson. (No NEED to be. Can you TALK?)

I RUN when I hear the words "business opportunity." (EVERYBODY does! *UGH!* I absolutely HATE that phrase, too.)

My wife will leave me if I try ONE more time with Network Marketing. (SNEAK at it and surprise her with a new Lexus for Christmas. She'll stay.)

And the objections go on, and on, and on. And do you know what? Most of these objections are **NOT valid!** MOST are just a way of not wanting to try, afraid to take a chance, remaining in a type of *comfort zone* forever. Do NOT allow ANYONE to discourage you!

What **I** would be more afraid of than anything, is knowing that I had to "exist" *my entire life* being BOSSED by somebody, having to PUNCH A CLOCK, and NEVER getting a taste of what it's like to be rich. So, let's look at it from a different perspective.

If you were in business for yourself and failed, let's talk about *why* it DIDN'T work and *how* it COULD have worked. Let's talk about some who have MADE IT who started at the beginning and those who came in long after the company began and STILL "made it."

If you are already IN a home-based business, I think I can help you become successful—or **more** successful. No matter how much money you are presently making, I'll tell you the *smartest* and *easiest* methods to make more.

And to those who are just "thinking" of getting into business for yourself, I will answer your questions truthfully and candidly and teach you HOW to do it CORRECTLY. In short, I give you the best CHANCE at being successful. I can't *guarantee* your success, only YOU can do that.

NEW TECHNOLOGY

You should NOT begin ANY business without using a computer. These aren't machines of the FUTURE; the *computer age* is upon us NOW. It does everything for you—even makes you rich. It can't THINK for you but it certainly HELPS you think. It can't choose the right business for you, but it helps you *manage* that business. It records, sends messages, takes messages, serves as a dictionary, thesaurus, almanac, weather reporter, it tells you about shows and show times, routes to travel by, it does just about EVERYTHING! It's not the NEW way of starting up a home-based business, it's the ONLY way.

SkyBiz 2000 is FEATURED because it's EXCITING! It is EASY to do, inexpensive to TRY, no need to be a genius, just follow "*the yellow brick road*" and if you work hard and smart, you can **BUY** Oz!

YOU HAVE A HOME-BASED BUSINESS

Many who are in a home-based business hit a *snag* once their *"warm market"* turns cold and soon becomes non-existent. New clients are tough to find. MY methods create a NEW warm market of strangers, all calling YOU to TELL them about whatever it is you are doing.

The most POPULAR home-based business is Network Marketing. It USED to be called Multi-Level Marketing but the name has changed; how it's done hasn't. *It's the same "church" just a different pew.*

MANY have been "burned" by an MLM or Network Marketing company in a variety of ways and I'll tell you how to have the BEST CHANCE of NOT being burned as well as WHY you failed a time or two (or three or four or, *Egad,* MORE), and how you can have the best CHANCE of winning THIS time.

Is it too late to "start all over?" *NO!* Is it too late to do it the RIGHT way? *NO!* Is there a NEW, EASIER way to become rich. Oh, Yes, YES, **YES!**

YOU FAILED BEFORE

SO WHAT? MOST millionaires failed in the past. *It isn't how many times you get knocked down, it's how many times you get* **UP!**

Oh, it's terrible to fail. Being poor is never good. But being poor, becoming RICH, and being poor *again* is devastating! Been there, done that. Now, I have several "secrets" that will prevent that "failing" stuff from ever happening to you (and me) ever again.

I'll share with you secrets that not only make *any* home-based business EASIER, but more profitable and much more FUN! You just have to read, understand, and BELIEVE!

I like people. I like it even *more* if people like me. I would *never* get in a business where I have to bother, badger, pursue, persuade, cajole, coerce, trick, beg, threaten or LIE to people to SELL them anything.

My dad once told me that *work, works*. He was wrong. My high school math teacher told me that ***hard** work, works.* He, too, wasn't *exactly* right. But my football coach had the answer; he said ***smart work**, works*. Well, *hard, smart work* can't miss!

How would you like to get rich with a small investment? With **NO** boss? **NO** college degree? **NO** sales ability? **NO** previous training? **NO** driving to and from work each day? **NO** childcare services to pay?

For a single parent, how nice it is to be *home* with your small children. Or AT home to greet your kids when they return from school. Being HOME is important for children during their formative years, but in these inflationary times it's often *necessary* that both parents work to survive.

Wouldn't it be nice if mom was at home? Wouldn't it be NICER if mom AND dad were at home? If you absolutely can't quit your present job, why not try a *part-time* job that could make you as much as you are making full-time? These are but some of the great advantages of a home-based business.

How about being able to TAKE OFF from work whenever *you* want, and to work as hard as *you'd* like knowing that the **more** you work the **more money** you make? Take off to see the kids play ball, take advantage of the vacation "deals" because you can leave ANYTIME. No need to dress up—even ***get*** dressed—if you choose not to. These are but *some* of the advantages of having your own business where you work out of your house.

The biggest advantage of working for yourself is that you can—with a *plan,* a *system,* and *dedication* —get rich, and make enough to guarantee a nice retirement for yourself and a comfortable life for those you love. Most can't do that working for someone else.

To be rich—to become a millionaire in ANY business—requires effort, time, smart thinking, planning, correct decisions, and perseverance. And LOT'S of work; hard, *smart* work!

EXPLAIN NETWORK MARKETING

I think the easiest way to explain Network Marketing is people talking with people, who talk with people, who talk with people, who talk with *more* people, etc. It's a whole line of people **telling** people about the product(s) or services they represent.

To begin, it's a *home-based business;* you are working for yourself. This means you don't need a store, newspaper or televison ads, or employees. You also have special TAX ADVANTAGES! Plus, some of the most successful network marketers I've met *never leave their homes.* They **DUPLICATE** their system and themselves. They get rich helping OTHERS get rich!

I learned how this duplication method worked when I read (somewhere) about a person who was hired to dig postholes for a large fence company. He was paid $10 a hole. No matter how hard or how fast he worked, it seems that 10 holes per day was his maximum. The most he could ever expect to earn was $100 a day. And, the company needed more holes dug for more fenceposts to remain in business.

So, this enterprising young man found five of his friends who needed a job and he hired *them* to dig holes for **$9** each. He showed them how to do it; he DUPLICATED himself. He still earned his $100 a day digging his own holes, but also $10 from each of his five employees or $50 a day extra from them. They did the same as he.

They each found five people (25 total) who were

digging 10 holes a day for $8 a hole. NOW, he earned his same $100 from his efforts, plus he was taking in $50 from his five workers, and he was NOW getting **another** $1 a hole times 10 holes from 25 workers or TWO HUNDRED AND FIFTY DOLLARS per day from *their* efforts.

To take it one step further, each of THOSE 25 hired five people each (jobs weren't plentiful then) to dig the same holes for $7 a day. Want to figure that out? I'll do it for you. He had 125 more hole-diggers earning him an additional $1 per hole times 10 holes or TWELVE HUNDRED AND FIFTY DOLLARS PER DAY! Just THINK if you had several THOUSAND digging holes for you. **THAT'S DUPLICATION!**

That little beginning hole-digger with NO money, just DUPLICATION, needn't dig any more holes. His job then was to watch over the diggers, cheer them on, and replace the ones who quit. He was taking in more than FIFTEEN HUNDRED DOLLARS a day! He began working *hard* and graduated to working *smart.* Here's another, almost unbelievable example of duplication.

Whether you play golf or not is unimportant; just know that there are 18 holes on a regulation course. Let's say someone talks to you about making a wager on a game. You agree to start with betting a PENNY on the first hole, doubling the bet all the way through. Seems safe enough, right?

The LAST HOLE plays for over THIRTEEN HUNDRED DOLLARS!

Don't believe it? Check it with your calculator. **That**, my friends, is the power of **DUPLICATION** and **that**, in a nutshell, is Network Marketing. **That** is how YOU can become rich. Learn, teach, and get others involved. You not only don't PAY them to work, but while you show them how to work for themselves, they are also working FOR you and they pay YOU.

A successful Network Marketing COULD make you wealthy and, at the very least, change your lifestyle to where you never have to read that menu *from right to left* ever again.

MANY people working **SkyBiz 2000 ON THE INTERNET** have upwards of **TEN THOUSAND** people digging holes for them. YOU can do it, too!

If you're the cautious type, work at it **part-time**. Then, when you start earning *three times* more than you are making at your present job—for more than six months straight—and you enjoy being in business for yourself, *quit* that regular job and do this full time.

KEEP THIS THOUGHT IN MIND:

"If you never TAKE a chance, you'll never HAVE a chance."

Chapter 2

HOW IT ALL BEGINS

Usually, it's when you are first *dragged* by a friend or relative to one of these "opportunity" meetings and there is some silver-tongued devil standing at the front of the room telling how you can earn $10,000 up to $50,000 a month (or more).

"*This is a bunch of bull,*" you say. But I've seen it happen over and over and OVER again by the most unlikely people one could imagine. Most looked as if they could never earn more than minimum wage.

For every person earning this kind of money after just 12 to 18 months, there are tens of thousands making $3,000 to $5,000 a month and more earning $1,000 or $2,000 a month. Many are only making expenses, and of course, MOST are *losing* money.

More people LOSE because they choose the WRONG product or service to work, they didn't know what they were doing in the first place, they had no business plan, or they were just plain lazy.

For those who *fail* in Network Marketing, it's easier to blame it on something or someone else. Thus, the entire industry gets a bad rap.

If you are SINCERE about making money, I

wholeheartedly recommend that you TRY Network Marketing. Just read this book with an open mind and forget what you've heard from others, or a failure or two you experienced in the past, because *that was then and this is now!*

Everything has changed and it is getting better as we breathe. If you *did* try and fail, perhaps you're not right for Network Marketing, or what you did was make some very *unwise* decisions.

PAST MISTAKES

Let's begin with those who were in Network Marketing two or three times (or more) and failed at it. Just to start with a clean slate, let's try to determine which of the following errors you were guilty of:

- **Became involved with the wrong company**
- **The wrong product**
- **You didn't work hard or smart**
- **You had no direction or training**
- **You didn't take time to learn and work the *system***

I know there could be other reasons for your failure, but these are sufficient for you to get the idea.

This book teaches you how to choose the RIGHT company, the RIGHT product, *and* how to earn BIG money. Additionally, you will know *exactly* what to expect from your efforts!

HOW MUCH CAN I REALLY EARN?

This, of course, is *impossible* to tell because we're all different. How much time, study and effort are you prepared to put into it? I can tell you that you *can* make **big** money in Network Marketing. I know hundreds of people, *personally,* who are making a **quarter of a million dollars a year** in less than **two years** in Network Marketing.

Do you know *how much money* that IS? If you're working for someone else, if you have a JOB, chances are you have no idea what I'm talking about. Ask yourself this. What could I do with that kind of money? *Answer:* You can live "the good life" FOREVER!

I know another who is earning at least a million dollars a year and he has been in **SkyBiz 2000** for only 10 months. And another doing *twice* that in the same amount of time. Do you SEE why I'm excited about this company? Are **YOU** excited?

Close your eyes and just dream. DREAM of riding in a new car that starts ALL the time. DREAM about coming into a new house, with a whirlpool bath and sauna, LARGE closets, NEW furniture, a huge kitchen, great landscaping, a private lake, private school for the kids, a MAID, and maybe even a COOK! Why not a personal valet? A BUTLER?

DREAM what you can do for your kids who might be old enough to go into business for themselves, or for your aging parents or grandparents. How THRILLED they'd be if THEY got a new house or a new car. And, **YOU CAN MAKE IT ALL COME TRUE!**

A MILLION DOLLARS A YEAR is within YOUR GRASP if you TRY with **SkyBiz 2000**. You might NOT make as much as one friend who is bringing in TWO million a year, but suppose you are HALF as good, or half THAT good or even half of THAT! That is still a quarter of a million dollars! Does THAT appeal to you?

Apply yourself, get in a habit of working a plan, set your goal and then *exceed* that goal. You have the OPPORTUNITY to TRY! You have a CHANCE to make all of this happen.

HOW DO THEY DO IT?

What makes these people different? Some have FAILED at other Network marketing companies. They didn't join this company at the beginning. They aren't all college educated; some had limited experience in ANY field. NONE are geniuses, and not ALL are salesman. They just saw an opportunity (that is STILL HERE, by the way) and they went for it.

I know a PIZZA DELIVERY BOY who, after less than two years in one company, was earning about a **quarter of a million dollars a year.** He could have CONTINUED delivering pizzas; he ATE well. But he TOOK A CHANCE and it paid off. Had he worked this hard in **SkyBiz 2000**, chances are he'd have been making TWO MILLION a year.

I met an 83-year-old BLIND lady who is earning

$7,000 a month in Network Marketing and by only "*watching over things*" (no pun intended) she will make more NEXT month.

A doctor friend of mine gave up his practice and works on patients' *pro bono* a few days each week; his main income is from Network Marketing. He ENJOYS helping others and by working only a few days a week, he now enjoys his work.

And remember, I'm not trying to *sell* you anything or interest you into joining any company; **I HAVE NO COMPANY!** My *business* is selling books and you already bought this one; I'm just trying to give you the secrets of making big money in an industry that is changing the way people buy things.

Now, think whom *you* know who is earning $250,000 a year or more—*legally? W*ithout a college degree, marrying into it, playing sports, being in the movies, winning the lottery, or who began their business with $110 and who hasn't been working most of their **life** at the same business.

I know a husband and wife team, both school teachers for more than 20 years, and their first year in Network Marketing they earned over $600,000. Had they applied this same effort to **SkyBiz 2000**, they very likely would have TRIPLED that! But *phooey* on them, they're already making it, let's talk about **YOU** and how **YOU** can do the same or better. Am I kidding you? **NO!** Is it REALLY possible? **YES!**

Here's how THEY did it. They had a plan. They worked hard, and they worked smart. They set a goal and went for it. They TRIED!

THE RIGHT PRODUCT

Without a doubt, the FIRST thing you look for is a *unique product or service* that nobody else has. It could also be something that almost everyone NEEDS (or wants) that is CHEAPER and/or can be delivered *faster* than a competitive product. To appeal to the majority, that product or service must make them:

- ☆ **Feel better**
- ☆ **Look better**
- ☆ **Live longer**
- ☆ **Save time**
- ☆ **Enjoy life more**
- ☆ **Save or MAKE them money**

The product is **vital!** Think about it. If the product is the same as *everyone else is selling*, what are your odds? It's smart to choose a product the MAJORITY wants or needs. Think of any number of PRODUCTS, ones that work, that are safe and legal—that **you** would be inclined to buy.

THE RIGHT COMPANY

At least three times a week I am called, faxed or e-mailed some new "business opportunity" that will make me rich. I'm already rich—or as rich as I need to be. And, I am NO Network Marketer; I'm a *teacher* of Network Marketing; I'm a coach, not a player. I'm in the book business, also the *people* business, and I market my books. I *NETWORK* all the time.

I had a plan, I worked hard and smart, I set a goal, and *I went for it.* I HELPED people help *themselves* and by doing this, they helped ME. That's the way I sell books. It's a *win-win-win-win* situation.

First win: The book helps sell the product. **Second win**: The people who *sell* the product make money. **Third win:** The company that *manufactures* the product makes money. **Fourth win:** I make money selling books. NOBODY loses!

Do you know that 87 of every 100 books you see in those large retail book stores go BACK TO THE PUBLISHER? And that the author of those 87% makes NO money? I often wonder, "How DO the publishers make money?" But **I** make money because I have a *unique* product, and I market it.

My company, for instance, (I'm known as a *small press publisher* because I only market a dozen or so different books a year as opposed to a few HUNDRED books) is *"one of,"* if not *"the,"* most successful in the world! I've lost on but three of the 177 books I've published.

One of my favorite sayings is, "**A MONKEY can WRITE a book, but it takes a TEAM of monkeys to SELL it!**" I choose my topics and my writers with care. I choose ONLY writers who are willing to WORK! Consequently, my percentage of successes is high. In fact, STAGGERING!

And when I tell YOU how to CHOOSE a company (after you choose the product) it's the same "secret" as I use in my business. I write what will entertain and/or sell. I find a PRODUCT that I *think* is good, I test it myself and if I like it, if I THINK it will appeal to a large majority, I market it.

I work HARD, but it does not *seem* like work! I get excited with success—with winning! As I said before, now, it's *the game!* AND, I **STILL** like to win but MY *winning* is trying to get OTHERS to know what it's like to live "the good life." I *absolutely* LOVE it.

I have *four secretaries* who handle only me and my work. But call, and chances are I'LL answer the phone. People WANT to talk with the one who wrote the book, to the *boss,* and they CAN.

I have a close friend, a world-famous medical doctor, his name is Ken Kroll. And when I call his number, HE answers the phone. I am always accessible and he, certainly more famous and more important than I ever *hope* to be, answers his phone and helps as many as he can help.

When people call me bursting with enthusiasm about their new product and/or company, and tell me how terrific it is, I listen. Of *course* it's the best, it's *their* chosen company—and chances are with this enthusiasm, they will *make* it work.

The first thing I need to know is *why* their company is the best. Exactly how much *research* has this excited caller done on the background of the company? On its officers? On the product? How *long* has the company been in business? What is their compensation plan? How many distributors does it have? Better yet, how *much* are these distributors *making* and, on average, how LONG have they been with this one company?

Chances are they know NONE of these answers. They attended a meeting and "heard" what the person in the front of the room told them and they liked the product and felt that they could sell it. And their *friend* who brought them to the meeting said it was *okay*. NOT GOOD ENOUGH!

FINANCIAL BACKING

Another factor to consider is, does the company have MONEY behind it? I do, however, know of several successful companies that began with a few people who pooled their credit cards and built a terrific organization, but for each one that succeeded, *tens of thousands did not!* Of ALL the companies that started on a shoestring, most ended up *hanging themselves* with that same string.

Research the company as best you can. There are many unexpected pitfalls in starting a new business and without *backup money*, if you make any number of mistakes along the way and if you don't have sufficient capital to "weather this storm," you are **OUT OF BUSINESS!**

COMPENSATION PLAN

On any job, one of the first questions you need to ask is, *How much money do I make? How do I get paid? When?* That's what you're really talking about. How much MONEY can you earn in this business and how long does it take to earn it?

SOME companies have distributors who work just as hard as others, but make far LESS with the same effort. GO WITH THE DOUGH! Check YOUR compensation plan.

The fact is, *most* Network Marketers *don't understand their own compensation plan* and couldn't explain it if their life depended upon it.

They get involved in a company because a friend *sells* them on the program and too much of the time the *friend* doesn't understand the compensation plan, either. MOST people are *naive*. Some are just really dumb. They WANT to believe that they can make a fortune working only three or four extra hours a week. IT HAPPENS THAT WAY ONLY IN DREAMS!

They hear someone give a good speech, the person who brought them *to* the meeting (whether they've heard the speech a *thousand* times or more) will sit next to them and smile and laugh at tired jokes they've heard over and over that simply cannot *still* be funny, and they get their friend to sign a paper and join and *then* they discuss the compensation plan.

If you just want to *buy* whatever they are selling and want to get it wholesale, sign and get the stuff and try it. But if you plan on it bringing income, FIND OUT what you're going to make and UNDERSTAND how it works BEFORE you make any blind commitment.

With **SkyBiz 2000**, there **ARE NO MEETINGS!** When there IS a meeting, it's more of an *event,* a *pep rally,* a FUN gathering people will **WANT** to attend. It is EASY to get people to go to THAT "meeting."

LEARNING and TRAINING

No matter how hard or smart you work, the first rule of marketing anything is that you KNOW what you're talking ABOUT. If not, how can you possibly tell others? You NEED to learn.

Read the literature, listen to tapes, watch videos, attend training sessions, and listen to what the one who sponsored you tells you. If you discover that they don't know what they're talking about or if they neglect you, go to the one who sponsored *them.* You NEED proper training!

INTEGRITY and ABILITY

The next "ingredient" is the INTEGRITY and ABILITY of the company's corporate officers. Without *qualified, experienced* officers with INTEGRITY, a company rarely becomes successful. You NEED corporate officers who KNOW what they're doing, who work hard, and who are *good* people. Where can you find all of this? It's out there. Know what to look for.

GREEDY or STUPID

Please don't fault me for my candor; this book is meant to help you, not insult you. What you can always expect from me is the truth and oftentimes there is not a delicate way to tell the truth.

The ONLY times I've lost on an investment was when I was either greedy or stupid—or both. I either thought I could *"make a killing"* with little effort or didn't do my homework. When I am going to invest time and money in anything, the first thing I do is *RESEARCH.*

I would have to believe that the individual introducing me to this new Network Marketing company was an intelligent person with integrity.

Also, I would have to SEE A NEED for the product and whether I could afford (or want) to take the *time required* to become involved. Then, I'd set goals (surmountable ones); still, DREAM big.

I know of people who are in SIX or EIGHT of these MLM, NM companies always TRYING to make "the big hit." Whereas, if you CHOOSE carefully your chances of the *big hit* is in ONE! Focus on ONE! Learn ONE! Find ONE that meets all the criteria I set down and THEN, when you have worked to a position that requires less of your time, either relax and enjoy what you've done or THEN look at a second one.

Yet another criteria for choosing a company to represent, is never worry about the NUMBER of distributors; this figure could be in constant flux. It is NOT an indication of how well a company is doing.

What I want to know about a company is not HOW MANY distributors they list, but . . .

✔ **How many CHECKS they pay out each month?**
✔ **What is the total pay out?**
✔ **How long they've been in business?**
✔ **How many of their *original distributors* do they still have since their first few years in the business?**
✔ **How many of their distributors make over $50,000 a year?**

With Network Marketing, please don't be sour on it because you failed a time or two (or three or four) in the PAST. READ what I've said and see if any of it fits your situation. I see far too many "regular" folks make **hundreds of thousands of dollars a year** when they find the right combination. Keep looking.

I am not the *rah- rah* type. I don't clap my hands, raise my voice and point, jump up and down with that *Go team Go, stuff.* I'm a "meat and potatoes guy" and I tell it straight. I'm telling YOU straight!

I get almost SICK when I see people working hard and getting nowhere. We can't ALL be bosses, but once we've "paid our dues" and saved some money, you owe it to yourself and your family to TRY and do better. TRY working for yourself. TRY to become a MILLIONAIRE!

Chapter 3
REALLY BIG MONEY

You will ALWAYS run into people who just *do not believe* in Network Marketing because of what they *heard*! Don't be offended by them, understand them and pray for them. *"They just don't know that they don't know*!"

Most are conservatives, or naive wage-earners, who have no *earthly conception* of HOW Network Marketing works, could never—not in their wildest dreams—reason that *anyone* other than movie stars, CEO's of giant corporations, star athletes, or *dope dealers* could make 10, or 15, or 20 THOUSAND dollars a WEEK! These folks you can *never* convince. Don't try! **Just don't listen to them!**

BIG MONEY

When I wrote the book titled, THE NEW MILLIONAIRES (the book that preceded this one) I wanted to help the "little" people earn an additional $500 or $1,000 a month working part-time. Because, even $500 extra a month will change the lives of maybe 95% of the people in the entire WORLD!

But in THIS book, I try to reach those of you who want to be **from RICH to FILTHY RICH**! And the **INTERNET** is the NEW way. I STILL want to help the "little" folks, but with this book I REALLY want to reach those who think BIG.

The little folks can make it, too, and become BIG! If you have no confidence in yourself of the power of the Internet, candidly, I don't want to waste my time screwing around with people who want to remain in a lower-middle-class income bracket. I've been poor and I've been rich, and poor—SUCKS!

What I hoped to do in that book was to SHOW these non-dreamers how EASY it is to make a few thousand here and there "playing" with Network Marketing, hoping that when they "tasted" this extra dough they'd go for more.

In THIS CHAPTER I want to address only the "players." I want people who not only dream BIG but who TRULY WANT to live a movie-star-type of life-style. That's why I got more and more excited while writing INTERNET MILLIONAIRES and why I'm "*pushing*" **SkyBiz 2000**; it **MAKES MILLIONAIRES!**

I know the people I am dealing with are bright if they understand, own, and work with a computer. I know they are going to make it if they just READ the information on **SkyBiz 2000** and realize what a TERRIFIC OPPORTUNITY this is for them to become wealthy beyond their wildest dreams!

I KNOW about numbers, about the millions who are going "on the Internet" every month, and this

matrix plan that NEVER FLUSHES, with a ⅓ to ⅔ **payout!** It's EASY to understand and EASIER to work! Maybe THIS IS THE TIME for me to jump up and down and clap my hands and yell *Go team Go!*

YES, I'm on a constant HIGH, for YOU! I have NEVER seen anything like **SkyBiz 2000** in the history of ANY Network Marketing company. It was FIRST and is getting stronger by the MINUTE!

I know, personally, more than three DOZEN people who were NOT successful in other Network Marketing ventures who "*learned from the bad*" and they NEVER QUIT! They turned it around and are making hundreds of thousands of dollars within MONTHS in ***SkyBiz 2000.*** I am thrilled FOR them.

I meet successful Network Marketers each WEEK who are driving luxury cars, living in *mansions*, and going on vacations for a *full month* only to return and find that they have *more money* in the bank than they had before they left!

I have a friend who QUIT a Network Marketing company where he was making about $200,000 a year, to get into **SkyBiz 2000.** Now, THAT was guts! I'd never recommend that. He calls me daily when people just "appear" in his downline.

"*Look at this. Look at that.*" He actually yells over the phone as he MAKES me punch up HIS computer screen and look at his **SkyBiz** genealogy.

"I don't even KNOW who these people are and they are joining under me faster than my odometer turns on the highway. Pete, this company is FANTAS-

*TIC! I've NEVER seen anything like it! I'll make at LEAST a million bucks in the next 12 months! Hurry with that book of yours!" (*I'm hurrying! I'm hurrying!)

Does Network Marketing really work? Does **INTERNET** Network Marketing work? **YES**, it does! Think those "wage earners" would believe that one of my friends is DISGUSTED with his business because he was *"stuck"* at $30,000 a month after just 17 months in Network Marketing? **BECAUSE**, he has a friend in **SkyBiz 2000** who has worked HALF that time and is making FOUR TIMES as much!

MANY Network Marketers who work smart and hard—who put in the hours and the time—are earning well over a MILLION dollars a year? If you told these *non-believer*s that, they would swear you were lying, crazy, or stupid. But, it's true.

The non-believers are, mostly, ones who *never take a chance.* They graduated from college, got a job, and that's all they know. They are either satisfied with their present job, or won't tell you if they're not.

Please don't make fun of them. They're EVERY-WHERE. Pray for them. No amount of convincing will alter their thinking, just pass them up. To prove that they REALLY don't know, they tell you that you are working a PYRAMID SCHEME.

PYRAMIDS

Let's put something to rest PERMANENTLY! Network Marketing **IS NOT** A *PYRAMID SCHEME*!

I can always spot a person who knows **ABSOLUTELY NOTHING** about this industry when they talk about a *pyramid!* But, bless their hearts, they *heard* of people losing in a "*pyramid scheme*" and they confuse it with Network Marketing.

First of all, the so-called "pyramid scheme" is ILLEGAL! The very first thing every assistant attorney general in any state looks for before the paint with their name on the door dries, is a company where people sell people something that involves *putting up money and no product is involved.*

The **only** ones who make money with these *schemes* are the ones at the top. Everyone else just *contributes*, and the LAST to join LOSES. THIS is where these unknowing folks got the idea that Network Marketing is the same. It is NOT!

Egyptians built the true pyramids; they started at the bottom and built UP. In Network Marketing, you build like the Egyptians; start at the bottom and work up. And, *yes*, Network Marketing IS work. I never even implied that it was *easy* work, I only promised you the OPPORTUNITY to make a lot of money with no prior credentials, a small investment, and to have a business of your own.

I WAS AGAINST NETWORK MARKETING

In 1980 I wrote a book on Multi-Level Marketing (former name for Network Marketing) and I *barbecued* the entire industry. The title was *The Truth About*

MLM, with a skull and crossbones on the cover along with **BEWARE** in large letters followed by several exclamation marks.

Because, I had known, and known *of,* so many who were led like sheep to the slaughterhouse into so many "get rich quick" deals involved with this type of selling. I warned of the pitfalls of MLM; the major ones no longer exist.

In that book of 20 years ago, I listed what was necessary to have a SUCCESSFUL Network Marketing company and now, today in the new millennium and starting in the early 1990's, there are many. You just have to know not only *what* to look for, but things to be wary *of.*

One large red flag (it's also ILLEGAL) is to *front load*—to have people *buy* their position by filling their garage full of products they can only *hope* to sell. Back then, many of the unknowing went bankrupt; they lost their car, their house, their savings and their family.

But, if you deal from your HEAD and not from greed or stupidity, you have a chance. That's what I plan to give you; the best CHANCE there is to be successful in Network Marketing.

EVERYBODY has the *best* plan, the *best* company, the *best* product, the best lawyer, doctor, dentist, tax accountant, spouse, etc., And THAT is one of the main ingredients in becoming successful in Network Marketing. You MUST BELIEVE in what you are doing.

STATISTICS

I'll not bombard you with statistics, because those aren't always accurate. It depends on *who does the survey.* Besides, I don't care what is happening in the financial world. My concern is what's going on in MY world—and YOURS!

I remember reading *statistics* when I was only a ten-year-old. Statistics like, "*America was prosperous and that the average American family was earning $10,000 a year.*" You understand, this was a *long time ago.* My father was earning $35 a week (BEFORE TAXES) and I don't want to add or multiply, but *that* was much less than $10,000 a year.

When the roof leaked from 20 different places in the two-bedroom shack we lived in and we ran out of pots and pans to catch the water, and we had to wait maybe *three paydays* to save the $7.50 for a roll of tar paper(that included the nails and a can of tar), *NO,* I didn't see **my** world as prosperous.

As a fun-loving 21-year-old there was more *statistics* that said, *"Ski Aspen! Guys, the women are* ***eight deep*** *at the bar."* I rushed to Aspen to ski. This was one time statistics were correct; women WERE eight deep at the bar, but MEN were TWENTY deep! So much for statistics.

I don't care how the Network Marketing statistics are documented. Let's make them better. Let's talk about what can be done to help you—NOW!

GROUND FLOOR OPPORTUNITY

That phrase is about as original as *"A bird in the hand is worth two in the bush."* I smile when someone tells me that, but in reality I could just about THROW UP! ONLY a *neophyte*—an amateur, someone NEW to the business—uses that terminology. **Ground floor opportunity! Get outta' here**! And, more likely than not, that person is poor and struggling.

HOW can someone who is *poor* tell others how to get rich? I want to hear how to get RICH from those who ARE rich! That's the same as the fat lady in the circus telling others how to lose weight. And that *bird in the hand* business is true, unless of course, you NEED **two birds!**

I know I've said this a time or two and I'll probably tell it to you a time or two more, but there is NO GUARANTEE in this business! Nor is there a guarantee in ANY business because there are a multitude of things that can go wrong. The main reason you fail, is YOU!

But, SHOULD you, "*Get in the company early; get in on the ground floor?*" The answer is SOMETIMES. But, MOST of the time it's often *smarter* to get into NEW companies AFTER the first year since so many never make it to that 12-month test! During the first year there will ALWAYS be changes and glitches; it's impossible *not* to have them.

From the *corporate* standpoint, there will be people to hire, people to fire, people to promote, new methods of telecommunication, new products and maybe a change in the marketing plan.

I remember a company I wrote a book about that boasted of over 200,000 distributors in two years. Many said "*They wish they had gotten in sooner.*" WHY?

NOW was the *best* time to get involved; MOST of the problems are solved, glitches are out, the company has a much better idea on what to expect, they have chosen the best people, their pay plan is stabilized, and they survived that first year! There are more than two hundred MILLION people in the U.S. alone, a hundred and NINETY-NINE million who had never *heard* of their product (OR yours). Just get in and CHARGE!

I remember when dozens of *Mom and Pop* shops in small towns were CLOSED because Wal*Mart moved in. These people had been doing business and earning a living for generations! And the neighborhood bookstores are fast disappearing because these giant stores with a MILLION books come in and offer discounts, serve *Starbucks coffee,* and are great social gathering places. I love these big stores. And, that's life!

Or some large company comes in and not necessarily a *hostile takeover* situation, but management changes and you get a *jerk* for a boss or you are laid off or forced into early retirement because of *downsizing*. How many of you have been victims of THAT terminology?

EARLY RETIREMENT! I'll tell you what THAT is! It means that you (probably) were given the option to *remain on* in your regular job and they would "put up" with you for a few more years. Or, take a *lesser retirement pay* and get out NOW. It's almost like being fired! It certainly (again, in most cases) makes you feel useless and unappreciated.

I don't want you to retire FROM something; I want you to retire TO something. Try Network Marketing *part time; play* with it; work it as many (or as few) hours as you choose. "Early retirement" usually means lesser pay and lesser benefits. And with prices of everything (except computers, VCRs and long distance telephone calls) going UP, you might NEED some extra income to live comfortably.

Early Retirement. Whew If you haven't saved or invested wisely, this means lesser comforts. It means YOU must *downsize* **your** spending. MOST Network Marketers are people over 50 who *are* retired. YOU know what I mean by all of this, don't you? Retire TO something. Chance are you'll earn MORE in your "retirement years" than you did the 40 or so years previously when you had a JOB!

So, take those negative friends, neighbors and relatives and do what YOU think is best. It's a time when you and your spouse can work together. And (again) not ALL NM companies require that you go to meetings but you can have fun at meetings, you can ENJOY meeting others just like yourselves.

Yes, my friends, why NOT be IN BUSINESS

FOR YOURSELF, working from your home, working leisurely and enjoying doing it? Network Marketing is the wave of the future. Fact of the matter, it's here NOW! So, jump on the bandwagon, just make certain it's playing the music you like.

MONEY ON THE INTERNET

You know of Bill Gates, and of Amazon.com, and maybe another half-dozen BIG names that are in the news. But did you know that in 1998 there was over 300 BILLION DOLLARS in business transactions in the United States alone over the Internet!

And that major publications like *Forbes* and *The Wall Street Journal* reported that, "Over the past 5 years, there have been more NEW MILLIONAIRES who were involved in **Internet businesses** than any other sector of the world's economy!"

THIS is why I am SHOUTING **SkyBiz 2000** to the rooftops! It not only *got* me excited, It KEEPS me excited. I get calls, faxes and e-mails daily on the new happenings from NEW MILLIONAIRES who made it in **SkyBiz 2000**. It has, in less than 12 months, changed the financial lives of THOUSANDS!

A THOUSAND DOLLARS A DAY is not uncommon with so many of those who write to me. Few are bragging; most are simply "OUT OF THEIR MINDS" WITH JOY!

SkyBiz 2000 has been in business a little over a YEAR! ONE YEAR! There are, according to my calculations, over THIRTY of their "distributors" earning $25,000 a WEEK—and MORE! In many OTHER companies, people who work JUST AS MUCH and JUST AS SMART, only a handful are making that kind of money.

In just about EVERY Network Marketing company there is *an Alien* who is earning near, at, or over a million dollars a year. Then maybe several who are making half that much. And following those, are several dozen making a few hundred thousand a year, or a bit more.

In **SkyBiz 2000** there are several HUNDRED making . . . the truth is, I don't know HOW MANY are making this BIG money. . . but it is SO big that I tell MY FRIENDS about it. In fact, I tell everybody I meet.

Now, I **DO NOT** solicit people for ANY company. I work for NONE, I sell PRODUCTS for NONE, and NONE are paying me. (Again), I just write books.

But, I OWE IT to those I care for, the same as if I discovered a cure for cancer or heart disease or any number of debilitating or fatal diseases, to TELL them about what I've discovered. That's what I'm doing with YOU through this book .

If I had a WAY to make EVERYONE in the WORLD become rich. I'd like that. I want to *expose* as many as I possibly can to the OPPORTUNITY to join **SkyBiz 2000**, and, as the title to the book reads, BECOME AN INTERNET MILLIONAIRE!

Chapter 4

WINNERS AND LOSERS

WHY COMPANIES FAIL

$ For a new state Assistant Attorney General making \$48,000 a year after graduating from college and then going to law school, it's not an *easy pill to swallow* when you hear of a retired school-teacher, an electrician who lost his business, or some former *pizza delivery boy* who are all making \$400,000 a year in Network Marketing, many of whom have never graduated from law school or even *been* to college . . . So, if there is but a *hint* of illegality, they move in and shut you down. That happened often a decade and more ago. But now, there are attorneys who specialize in setting up Network Marketing companies and this rarely happens any longer.

$ In the back of the *contract* you sign for MOST Network Marketing companies (perhaps printed in small letters because they have a lot to say and limited space to do it) there is a clause that states "*the company has the right to change their compensation plan (even some of their rules) whenever THEY choose*" (or something to that effect). This means that the COMPANY, if their officers so vote, can CHANGE your *pay* without you having anything to say about it! It happens often, and almost ALWAYS results in a *reduction* of pay.

If this happens *after* you are involved, *after* working and adjusting to a comfortable lifestyle, you have two choices; *stay in and bite the bullet, or LEAVE.*

I've seen this occur *many* times over these years with companies who either didn't know what they were doing and *had* to change their pay plan (*rarely* in favor of the distributor) to survive, or the ones who run the company get greedy.

They become so enamored with their own self-worth, they believe all the wonderful things their distributors say about them, they see the lifestyles change for so many, they become so arrogant that they feel they can do as they choose, and the distributors will stay.

WRONG AGAIN! When they take MONEY away from their distributors, the distributors leave! And, they leave in *hoards* causing the entire organization to crumble.

$ MOST Network Marketing companies fail the first year because of *under-funding.* The lack of BACKUP MONEY is number ONE, because there are so many errors that can be made that only money gives you the *staying power* to remedy.

The second reason is a *toss up* whether the

corporate officers or the distributors cause the failure. Let us start at the top with the . . .

$ *Corporate officers* who can't handle the pressure. Some are not bright. They might hire someone (usually from a failed company) who brings stale ideas and antiquated systems. I can't understand that one.

IF a company starts to *slide,* it takes a substantial bit MORE of hard, smart work AND money to rescue it, and if they do not recognize the slide in time, the outcome is its demise.

To run ANY business, it takes a great product, money, experience, talent and hard, SMART work. Without competent guidance, along with a product people need or want, it never works.

$ *Distributors* are the number ONE REASON for Network Marketing companies failing. If *any* company has 50,000 or 100,000 or more representatives, chances are high that there will be **some** *fruit cakes* in the bunch. With many of the top Network Marketing companies in healthcare products, it's their *distributors* who exaggerate or lie to make a sale.

There are *governmental regulatory agencies* established to protect the consumer from fraudulent claims and misrepresentations by companies. More often than not, *the company* is not at fault; their *Independent Distributors*, from greed, stupidity or both, cause the COMPANY to be fined or closed down.

That is why companies REFUSE to allow their *distributors* to appear on TV or talk over the radio or make statements in newspapers. If that DISTRIBUTOR makes one slight error, the company and all the other distributors suffer.

How can you stop this? **You can't!** It's human nature and *Murphy's Law* comes into play often. I've seen (recently) several promising and large NM companies close their doors or lose 75% or more of their distributors because of some dumb statement made by one of their distributors.

Oh, the distributor who is the *culprit* is "sorry" for their stupidity or greed, but tell THAT to the tens of thousands of distributors who can't make a mortgage payment or put food on the table.

$ IF the COMPANY changes the *compensation plan* and *lowers* the commissions of their distributors —*certain death!* This is what usually happens.

Those who were making $20,000, $30,000 (and MORE, per month) if cut by as much as *half*, still stay in because they had never made that much money before in their lives. So, they *bite the bullet.*

BUT, the "little folks" who were making $2,000 or $3,000 per month (who usually comprise about 75% of the total distributors) if *their* income is cut in half, they can't live on $1,000 or $1,500 per month, and they *have no choice* other than quit, go back to their regular, salaried job or look elsewhere to survive. It breaks both their pocketbook and their hearts. Yes, it REALLY hurts *that* group most.

And when *they* leave, it isn't long before those who were making the **big** money will be cut even more. It doesn't happen overnight! But it happens. Sometimes it takes four months or six months to catch up, but it WILL, and ultimately, it is *goodbyville* for that company.

The company could experience buyouts, hostile takeovers, changes in management, in policy, etc. Even though there is NO DIFFERENCE in "regular" companies, when this happens in a Network Marketing company, EVERYBODY knows of it and talks about it.

Friends and families seem to take a certain satisfaction and say "I *told you so*" and thus, the bad rap against the entire industry. That's just the way it is! MANAGEMENT IS EVERYTHING!

I have a neighbor, Nolan Ryan, one of the best pitchers ever to play the game of baseball. When he was with the Houston Astros, he had the lowest ERA in the league, but he lost too many games because m*anagement* didn't get the players who could hit the ball. Nolan would have had to pitch a *no-hitte*r to even *tie!* Sometimes he gave up two or three hits and LOST the game. Sometimes, one hit.

And management let him go to the Texas Rangers where he went on to pitch a few more no hitters and end up in the Baseball Hall of Fame. *Management is for management*. Smile, be friendly with them but look out for yourself. Nobody else will. It happens many times to many people.

Conversely, if *you* get a better deal, you are gone, too. So *your* loyalty is to *your* business and yourself and your family; their loyalty is to themselves and their family. That's life as it is, and not for the dreamers, idealist or the naive.

$ No matter WHAT you invent, concoct, formulate or discover, SOMEBODY will try to capitalize on it, *copycat* it, and sell it cheaper, get it to you faster, promise a better pay plan, or offer more amenities and you *go for it.* It happens every day.

I remember the *Health Rider*, that rowing-type exercise machine that you sit on and exercise using your own body weight. A friend of mine, Lloyd Lambert whose shop is about 10 miles "down the road" from me, invented it. It sold for about $500 and Covert Bailey, best-selling author of *Fit or Fat* was their primary spokesman. The company made a fortune.

Within minutes of the TV campaign, about five *other* machines appeared on the market, some selling for less than $100. The hundred-dollar model wasn't as sturdy or attractive, but it sold and hurt the *Health Rider* sales immeasurably.

This happens in ALL businesses. If somebody else has the *same thing* that is cheaper (or *almost* the same thing)people go for IT. That is why I say to choose a company who has a UNIQUE product that *nobody* can copy or sell cheaper, and go with them. OR, find a company that has such a head start that copycats will rarely or NEVER equal.

JUMPERS

In *every* Network Marketing company there are those who do not do well and go over to another company hoping to do better. Most *don't* do better! If they fail in San Francisco, chances are they'll fail in Tallahassee.

With Network Marketing companies, you must work the SYSTEM! You must WORK! It is, without doubt, the FASTEST (legal) way to get rich. But, have no doubt about it, it IS work! Those who work make it, and those who don't work DON'T make it. *Jumping* to another company has *rarely* been the answer; the answer is looking back at you in the mirror.

Regardless of the company you're representing, "things" will never always go YOUR way. If you are overlooked for an award, so what? If your upline doesn't help you, so what? If they hire someone in corporate you don't like, so damn WHAT? This won't affect your PAY one cent. Grow up! NOTHING will ALWAYS go *your* way regardless of what you do. That's life!

Jumping companies is like jumping from a high diving board when you were a kid. Once you jump, it gets *easier to do* a second time, and a third, and so on. And there are just so many people who will follow you. Some "close friends" will stay with the company. Where MONEY is concerned, friends go with the money. And they SHOULD or their family suffers.

Some, of course, *will* follow you. Then, there are those who *see* you jump and they will NOT follow and will lose faith in whatever you say. They feel if you "jump" once, you'll jump again. It really isn't fair to them, but jumpers always want to take their downline with them.

Decide on ONE company and GO TO WORK! Stay focused on that ONE company! IF, of course, you made an educated choice. Unless something really MAJOR goes wrong, do NOT jump.

WORK FOR TWO COMPANIES

I have no set rule for doing it or for *not* doing it because people have different talents. This is a tough call BECAUSE most companies want you to work *only for them*! Their reasoning is both simple and subjective, and they are RIGHT (most of the time).

Most people cannot FOCUS on more than one product or service. You cannot wear a variety of *hats*. You begin to look like the *boob* in a small town who is grocer, postmaster, fire chief, sheriff, and mayor. You simply cannot do *all* of these jobs EFFECTIVELY, and you end up making a little here and a little there and it NEVER comes out to be what you *could have made* if you worked ONE job, with ONE company, and gave it your all.

A company doesn't like distributors who represent them working a *second* company because if you're a leader, the other distributors will do as you do (most CAN'T do two things well at the same time) and everyone loses. They certainly don't want you "recruiting" other members into your *new* company; that takes from *their* pocket. Many have rules in their contract that forbid such a happening.

A second company *might* be considered when you feel you have "peeked out" with one company's pay plan and distributors under you are keeping your income at a certain level. Even then, you must be available for leadership and moral support to your downline.

ANOTHER reason you *might* try to work more than one company is if you feel that your *primary* company is on shaky ground and you want INSURANCE against them going out of business. If the company *does* go out of business, the corporate officers rarely leave broke.

They had warning of it happening and they *stored their nuts.* You don't want to be left, all of a sudden, without a job. So, *squat* what *the company* wants, think about what is best for YOU.

If the company folds, chances are you'll never hear of or see the corporate offices ever again. They are either looking to start ANOTHER company, or they are living on a beach in the tropics. MY concern, as well as YOUR concern, is for YOU. This book is meant to help YOU, not some company!

Oh, I'll come under fire for this one, because professional Network Marketers will tell you: "*Two companies are like having two wives,*" the men will say. "*It's difficult handling one.*"

A J.O.B. vs. AN OPPORTUNITY

Working for a SALARY is called earning **"linear"** income. You make so much and you will NEVER make more unless you work overtime, or you work harder or faster (FOR someone), and you'll NEVER get rich. That is a J.O.B.

With Network Marketing, you build **"residual"** income, the ONLY way to get rich. You **duplicate**; you *network;* you work a *system* that after you've trained others to do as you, you can go off on vacation and when you return you have *more money* in the bank than you had before you left. THAT is FUN!

Multi-Level Marketing got a bad rap because you always HEAR THE BAD. Newspapers sell on BAD news. And the very LETTERS, MLM, made so many people wary that they changed it to *Network Marketing* and now to HOME-BASED BUSINESS. *Same church, different pew.* BUT, if you want a CHANCE to make BIG money with a little investment, call it what you like, just DO IT!

Usually, the person who lives the *most comfortable* lifestyle is the one who has or had ONE job and stayed with it for a long period of time. That goes if you're working for someone, or if you're working for yourself. You alone can make that call. I'm just telling you some things to be aware of.

THE SYSTEM

All Network marketing companies will have their own system. USE THEIR SYSTEM! It was designed only for *that* company and *that* product, but it works on just about ANY Network Marketing company.

Many people try to "*reinvent the wheel.*" They will sit behind their computers and write, and printout, and SEND this "new" system to others and unless they are experts in their field, they are going to only CON-FUSE people.

Go to WORK, fella! Use what you have. It's worked for many before you and will work for many after you. You can always modify the system to sort of *tailor-make* it for you, but spend your time recruiting and training others to do likewise.

HAVE I GOT A DEAL FOR YOU!

Yes, **every *day*** I get at least two calls from people wanting me to join this company or that company and each of their companies is *the very best.* Or they have some NEW and UNIQUE product. EVERYBODY is trying to get rich, and I applaud them for it.

You've been approached too, haven't you? Time and time again, right? I say this to all who call and want to interest me in their new idea or company.

"Let's make a deal. I'm not trying to be rude and I'll listen for TWO minutes and if it SOUNDS good I'll listen more. But ONLY if at the end of two minutes and

I say 'No thanks,' you agree to change subjects, ask about my health, tell me about yours, let's have lunch or play golf."

And, I am sent free "*stuff*" all the time. I have a box of wrinkle patches, water from Okinawa that does something-or-other, cartons of various vitamins of which "*there is nothing like them in the world,*" boxes of anti-aging solutions, powders and pills, a machine that vibrates you like a snake, finger springs that cure most ills, a magnet for my pillow, some blue ointment that you put on a sore back and run a line to each side of your hip, and Viagra-type sex pills.

If I take them ALL, I'll gain weight. If I USE them all, I'll have no time to do anything else. Yeah, stick with ONE thing and work it IF you believe it and have checked it out thoroughly.

Talk to those who are trying to interest you and look at THEIR checks. Look at those who ARE making big money and you'll decide that, "*If THEY can do it, **I** can't miss!*" Take a chance, just don't invest too much money that will "hurt" if you lose.

So WHAT if you try and fail? At least you TRIED! I think it's worse *not* to TRY. Of COURSE you'll make mistakes. Who doesn't? I've written about 60,000 words in this book. Chances are HIGH that I'll make six or eight typos, leave a word out here or there but, again, so WHAT? Ever make 60,000 decisions and be *wrong* only six or eight times?

The ONLY **guarantee** is YOU! Too many things can go wrong that no *one* person can control. Work hard, work smart, be alert and make a LOT of money. You truly CAN in Network Marketing.

Network Marketing is no different from any other business—EXCEPT—you can make *more money* in it with such a small investment.

THINGS YOU MUST DO

I'm about 80% efficient, but that's not enough. If you plan to earn BIG money, find someone who is maybe 80% also, but *their* eighty covers the twenty you lack.

Another thing is, you *need* to be (or get) *ORGANIZED*. One of the basic rules for being in business for yourself is TIME MANAGEMENT. Your *time* is your income; try to spend it wisely.

PAPERWORK

Despite the *number* of people you recruit and sponsor, or how much *product* you sell, it must be properly RECORDED. Make certain you know **exactly** how to do it or all your efforts will be lost.

If you are not the type who can "keep things in order," either get a COMPUTER, or ask your spouse, mother, sponsor or somebody. Who knows? You might even recruit your *helper* to become active in your *downline*. After you learn to correctly fill out the paperwork, you need to keep track of your progress; you need to fully understand about . . .

VOLUME

People certainly count, but GOOD people count more. I've seen some *lucky* Network Marketers who enrolled only five or ten people and they are making hundreds of thousands of dollars per year. Then, I've seen some who had *thousands* of people and they were making schoolteachers' pay. It isn't "warm bodies" or names, it's the VOLUME of sales that count in ALL Network Marketing companies that involve product.

The really TERRIFIC thing about SkyBiz 2000 is there IS no product to buy, carry around or store. The COMPUTER does all your paperwork and you NEED NOT BE PRESENT when you sign someone up. There are no VOLUME REQUIREMENTS and it is actually THE easiest network business I have ever seen or heard about.

PROSPECTING

Finding people to recruit for your downline is called PROSPECTING. Just for the heck of it, list everyone YOU KNOW. You'll be surprised to find that you will end up with several *hundred* names—or more.

You are now in the PEOPLE business, and the more people you talk to the better your CHANCES of being successful. Network Marketing is the LEAST EXPENSIVE way I know of to be in business for yourself, and the ONLY limitations you have are your own desire and effort to make it work.

THE THREE-FOOT RULE

This means that when anyone comes within *three feet* (or is it TWO feet?) of wherever you are, you tell them about what *you're* marketing. This works for some and *scares the daylights* out of others. If you want to give yourself another method to meet and recruit people, do it. It works. Most of the successful Network Marketers *swear* by it. At least try it.

Look around you. There are truly pleasant people in the world. If you have a brochure, stick it in their hand as you pass by. They won't hit you or cuss at you. They might even *call* you if your brochure interests them. The very worst that will happen is that they'll toss it on the ground. Then, somebody else might pick it up and call. EFFORT pays off.

FOLLOW UP

Whew! Is THIS important? After you make contact with a person, call them within a few days and FOLLOW UP! If you don't follow up, *you fail.* It's that simple. They need to know that you are interested enough in what you're doing to find out how THEY are doing. Please, FOLLOW UP.

It is a known fact among professional sales people that very few sales are made from an *initial contact* alone. If you ask the top salesperson in any field, "What is your ***best*** sales technique?" They will reply with two words, "FOLLOW UP!"

RECRUIT and SPONSOR

When you *recruit* a person, you just sign them up. *Marines* recruit. They talk to some kid fresh out of high school and tell them all the wondrous things about being a Marine.

Those "*recruiters*" are dressed in their pressed uniforms with all sorts of medals pinned over their left (and now even the right) breast pocket. They are just that: Marine ***RECRUITERS***. They do what "*recruiters*" do; "*enroll*" the kids, turn them loose, forget them and never see them again.

When you *SPONSOR,* you become responsible *for* that person. TEACH them the business. Teach them how to *teach*. Show them the best way to become successful. Teach that person what **duplication** is. You are building your business by *showing them* how Network Marketing works. Once they are trained properly and really see it in action, they will go out and do the same thing.

Chapter 5
MARKETING

Marketing is the *only* way to move your product or service. Getting "the word out" to people is necessary. The question is, *How to do it in the least expensive way and get the best results*? Below is a fun example of smart marketing.

About 50 years ago in Louisiana, there was a man named Dudley LeBlanc who began a magnificent marketing campaign for his product called *Hadacol.* I don't even think *Amway* was around then.

He sent over a dozen telephone solicitors into Atlanta, New Orleans, Dallas and Houston. (These were supposedly the *most difficult* southern cities to sell anything new.) Each worker was told to sit in their hotel room and call the various pharmacies and grocery stores (before supermarkets and WAY before the computer) and ask if they had *Hadacol* in stock. The question always came back; "*What's Hadacol?*" And they were **told**, not **sold**.

After a week of making hundreds of calls a day each, they changed cities and began the calling again. The calls went on for a solid month. Then, in comes a band playing *The Hadacol Boogie* followed by dozens of trucks loaded down with *Hadacol.*

The merchants rushed to get their *allotted* cases of *Hadacol.* Some paid extra *under the table money* to truck drivers to get double and triple the amount LeBlanc set for them. These store owners WANTED the *Hadacol* because they convinced them that their *customers* wanted it; they had so many calls ASKING for *Hadacol.*

I even remember a verse or two of their songs.

"The rooster and the hen were sittin' in the shade.

The hen did the boogie while the rooster layed the egg.

He did the Hadacol Boogie, the Hadacol Boogie, the Hadacol Boogie makes you Boogie Woogie all the time."

The store owners lined their shelves with lots of *Hadacol* and put up huge signs. When the customers saw this *humongous* display, they bought *Hadacol.* Everybody loved *Hadacol;* it was said to have cured a multitude of ills. Later it was discovered that it was 33% alcohol. No WONDER it made people feel good; if they drank enough, **they all became intoxicated!**

I'm not certain of the accuracy of the *Hadacol* scenario, whether my dad told me what was true or what he believed to be true, but I remember that song. (When we meet, ask me to sing a verse for you). So, whether or not this is exactly how it happened is irrelevant; that's MARKETING.

Another example of marketing I recall hearing about was when the first *sardines* were introduced to Americans. A company canned PINK sardines. The problem was, pink sardines were very rare whereas WHITE sardines were plentiful.

The public's demand for these pink sardines was so great that the fishermen couldn't catch enough of the smelly little pink type. A new company emerged and tried to sell WHITE sardines. Consumers wouldn't buy them; they wanted the PINK delicacies.

That's when some marketing genius wrote a powerful message on the can of WHITE sardines.

GUARANTEED NOT TO TURN PINK IN THE CAN

INTERNET MARKETING

This is FAR different than **ANY OTHER** Network Marketing in existence! It is **EASIER**. It is **FASTER.** It is more **THOROUGH.** And **MOST** of what people don't like about Network Marketing is **NOT INVOLVED.**

First, you can SIT HOME BEHIND YOUR COMPUTER and work with it and a telephone. You can "reach" people through your e-mail and that is FREE (for now, anyway! Congress is trying to put a *toll* on e-mail letters). Since **SkyBiz 2000** is an Internet business and mostly what this book is about, let's talk about it.

You need **NOT** keep notes. EVERY transaction involving **SkyBiz 2000** is done ON the computer and you have NO PAPERWORK to keep, you do NOT FILL OUT AN APPLICATION by hand; **everything** is recorded by the new distributor on their computer which is all sent directly to the company and you have a record of that, instantly, on YOUR computer.

There's no need to do bookkeeping; it is done on your computer. You don't have to LUG any "stuff" around; there IS no stuff! It's all ON THE COMPUTER!

As far as MARKETING, every one you know who has a computer can be sent a short message. "LOOK at - - - - - - -(whatever your web site is named). Tell me what you think." THAT'S IT!

When someone sends YOU a message, reply with YOUR message. Make up some cards."BECOME AN INTERNET MILLIONAIRE" and put your e.mail address and maybe your telephone # on it and HAND IT OUT TO EVERYONE YOU GET CLOSE TO. Send it to relatives, friends, neighbors, EVERYBODY YOU KNOW.

USE ME AND MY BOOK

Once you join **SkyBiz 2000**, I'll work with you because I believe in it so passionately. I'LL do radio shows for you— **FREE**. I'll make conference calls with and for you—**FREE**. Plug me into any "gatherings" you might have. Again, **NO CHARGE**. Get me to your meeting SITE and I'll "knock them down" for you and again, **FREE**! Let me explain.

First, *most* people think an author is kind of special. I'm not, but **LET THEM THINK THAT!** In fact, *encourage* that thinking. It gets me on these radio shows where I advertise FOR YOU—**FREE!**

MOST people feel if it's written in a book, it's SO. In my case it IS true! And, since I'm a *third party* (don't work for the company or sell the product) they BELIEVE me.

Radio stations *all over the world* interview authors with new books. What a great topic, **BECOME AN INTERNET MILLIONAIRE**, with a sub title of How To Succeed in a Home-Based Business. Almost EVERYBODY wants to work for themselves, and more than that would like to be wealthy.

YOU write to ANY radio station with a talk format, and send a short note to the program director or host (both) along with a PROFILE of me, and wait. If they don't call, call them back in five or six days and ask if they got your correspondence. If *Yes*, send them a copy of the book and set a time.

I'LL do the show (done thousands and I'm good at it), talk about home-based businesses, MENTION **SkyBiz 2000** and then, the kicker. *"For everyone who would like to FIND OUT how to get a FREE BOOK, call this number."* Then I give out YOUR number and (I'll even record MY VOICE on your answer machine) YOU get the calls.

One lady in Ohio signed up 81 distributors in her

NM company in three weeks. Another distributor received over 300 calls in three weeks. There are more stories, but when you e-mail me and ask for my **SKYBIZ INFO PACKET**, you'll learn it ALL. That, too, is FREE!

It's 10-pages long and I'll mail it to you or e-mail it instantly. Does it work? One company I wrote a book somewhat like this one, sold over 65 MILLION dollars of product in about 20 months from those who called their distributors for a FREE book!

Yes, the book is an EXCELLENT marketing and sales tool! I report FACTS, I "*tell it like it is*," and the book is in BIG print, SMALL words, and can be read in one sitting.

SkyBiz 2000 is a "dream come true" for so many. It's *terrific* for those who understand the Internet. It's *awesome* for those who are learning about the Internet. It's SPELLBINDING for those who understand how to MULTIPLY. And it's EASY!

It features a two-sided payment plan that NEVER flushes, a one-third, two-thirds payout for volume, and the potential is unlimited. Not like a JOB. With a job the ONLY way to make MORE is to work harder, faster or longer hours. If you do that with **SkyBiz 2000**, you'll (probably) BECOME AN INTERNET MILLIONAIRE.

At the end of this book there will be a **NUMBER TO CALL** for information on **SkyBiz 2000.** The number is of someone (**SkyBiz 2000 member**) who will GUIDE YOU to a computer web site where you can peruse the information and make up your own mind. They will then call you back (if they read my book); remember, FOLLOW UP!

If you say *yes*, they will HELP you. If you say *no,* they are *instructed* NOT to bother you again. They will not try to SELL you. This book SHOULD do that and if it doesn't, my feelings are that:

1. You don't understand the internet.
2. You are not willing to TRY.
3. You aren't interested in working for yourself.
4. You are satisfied with your JOB.
5. You have no desire to be rich.
6. You are ALREADY rich.

"*Money isn't everything; a guy with 78 million is no happier than a guy with 75 million.*"

Chapter 6
METHODS TO WIN

MEETINGS

I know, you *hate* going to meetings and you have tried and *tried* to get your friends to go and it is next to impossible to get them there. There are NO MEETINGS with **SkyBiz 2000.**

If you are invited to HEAR about **SkyBiz 2000,** it's an EVENT, a PARTY, a GATHERING of people who are either financially successful or trying to be financially successful.

Meetings, like them or not, are the LIFEBLOOD of every Network Marketing company. Meetings are the *best way* to increase your business. Period. But, you don't NEED to attend meeting with **SkyBiz 2000** —only if you WANT to—and these meetings are special, they are DIFFERENT.

You LEARN at meetings. If you HATE meetings, use them as TRAINING SESSIONS. *Learning* is of vital importance in any business. You learn from the person conducting the meeting and you learn from others present *at* the meeting. SOME people LIKE meetings; I LOVE them!

GETTING FRIENDS to MEETINGS

The second you invite even your best friend to an "*opportunity meeting*" an *invisible wall* appears that even *Superman* can't break through. Most have heard of an opportunity meeting and they don't want an *opportunity! So,* PLEASE, don't call it that.

People LIE to **not** go to a meeting. They know you're going to try to get them to sell make-up, soap, vitamins, floor polish, invest in a bank in the Cayman Islands, or go in with them in a timeshare condo with 50 others for your one week per year in *Afghanistan*.

Even if they (finally) *agree* to have you *pick them up at their home*, there have been instances where the ENTIRE FAMILY turns out all the lights and lies *face down on the floor* afraid to breathe, with hopes that you stop ringing their doorbell or pounding on their door. They'll make up a good lie for you in the morning once they've had time to think about it.

Please *don't deceive* them pretending you're inviting them out to eat or to a movie. I've found that the best approach is to ask them to accompany you as a personal favor to you as you'd rather not go alone.

OR, *"Joe, you're my friend. I'm thinking of getting involved (or ARE involved) in a new company and I'd like to you to come with me and tell me WHY or WHY NOT I shouldn't go with it."* Slick, huh? And not *entirely* untrue. And, you *might* Get Joe to join once he hears the presentation.

With **SkyBiz 2000**, being it's so new and with so

many making really BIG money, it is EASY to get people to go with you. It's different, it's EXCITING, it 's the INTERNET! As you read through this, MOST of what many HATE about OTHER Network companies is not involved in **SkyBiz 2000.**

I know dozens of individuals who join just to *attend the meetings,* and never CARE if they make money. This is their *thing.* Bless them, but don't waste your time WITH them if you are money oriented because they will never do anything but help fill a room and enjoy themselves.

If you invite (or take) your new guest to a FUN meeting, chances are that guest will bring a *new* guest with them the *following* week. This is a great method to create your *downline* organization and build your business in ANY Network Marketing company.

Getting a new person to a meeting *every week* is difficult. After a year there is nobody left. WHO has 52 FRIENDS (neighbors and relatives) they can drag to a meeting? After a while that "warm market" is stone COLD!

If it's a friend, relative or a loved one, you *owe* it to them to share your good fortune, to help them find something that might change their lives for the better. If you **believe** in what you're doing, so will they.

But, I would (personally) never BADGER anyone to do something they are against. And with **SkyBiz 2000,** you have an option. Hold a meeting if you feel it will work. If it doesn't, FORGET the meeting; work on your computer, telephone and those three-way calls.

MY SUGGESTION is: TELL and NEVER sell! I feel that with **Internet Marketing**, you have a higher echelon of people to work with. They are *bright*, they are *aware*, MOST have a DESIRE to do more with their life, and **MY BOOK** does the selling. If they read the book and they aren't interested in Internet Marketing and/or **SkyBiz 2000**, pass them UP!

Remember, "*You can't teach a pig to sing. You waste your time and aggravate the pig.*"

I absolutely HATE the way the *Amway* people recruit; they *never* tell you WHAT the meeting is about until you're there a half hour or so before they spring this "business opportunity" *stuff* at you. I HATE being deceived, and *they train their reps* to do it that way.

Johnny Carson, just before he retired from late-night televison, said, "*I don't care if they get rid of the* ***dope dealers*** *from the streets, what I'D like is for them to get rid of the Hare Krishna's and the Amway salesmen.*"

HOME MEETINGS

ANOTHER advantage of **SkyBiz 2000!** You truly cannot WASTE TIME talking with one or two or even ten people AT THEIR HOMES. If you want to reach the MASSES, work on your computer. When I do a radio show FOR YOU, for example, this gets people who at their home calling YOU at YOUR home.

You do NOT have to DRIVE to their house, and they don't have put their house "in order" for your visit. It is fast, trouble-free, and you accomplish TWENTY TIMES MORE over the telephone or over your computer. It's the NEW way of Network Marketing!

THREE-WAY CALLS

I SHOULD take *pages* to talk about this method of working your business, but I won't. You bright folks will understand how POWERFUL this works for ANY type of Network Marketing and ESPECIALLY for working **SkyBiz 2000.** I can think of NO BETTER METHOD! It is EXCELLENT! Use them often.

Using the telephone is THE most important part of Network Marketing. You can "talk to" dozens in the time it takes you to drive to or visit ONE. The *most successful* Network marketers live by their phone and their computers. It is THE BEST WAY so sponsor new people!

CONVENTIONS

Conventions are the best **AND THE MOST FUN** to attend. If you can entice a person you want to sponsor to a *convention*, they WILL be impressed. The speakers are usually chosen for their ability to communicate and they are the *elite* of the company. They are the ones who know how to "make things happen."

The highest income earners aren't necessarily the best speakers. If they aren't, give them an award, shake their hand, pat them on the back, have them wave and smile at the audience, then SIT DOWN!

At the general assembly of a convention, the focus needs to be on FUN, MOTIVATION, and in getting the people *pumped*. Don't TEACH. Teach at the breakout sessions. That way, if the speaker is dull, you can gently slip out or just be in for a limited time.

NEW FRIENDS

I have met *many* truly wonderful people while researching this Network Marketing business. They are all *"so alive"* and always doing things. It's like one huge club, and when they have large meetings, it reminds me of a high school reunion. I dedicated my book to Network Marketers from *everywhere*!

Because of my books, I have become a part of a large Network Marketing *"family."* My books have helped change the lives of many, and I feel really good about myself because of it. I actually LOVE to sit around a table of Network Marketing people and listen to their enthusiasm about their products or services.

Some are rich and some are not. There isn't a *class barrier* of any kind, although their are *cliques,* the same as in any school, club, etc. The BIG money earners know each other and the *little* money earners know (or know OF) the ones who make the big money.

The big money folks are announced at the

conventions and are featured in the monthly magazine or newsletter. It's the same as the guy in school who scores the most touchdowns or the gal who is selected as homecoming queen. Want to be known? Want to be a winner? Succeed, too!

Do I LIKE Network Marketing? **I LOVE it!** Because of the people in it and because if you work it smart, you truly CAN change your financial life. I say TRY Network Marketing; mingle with those who *are making things happen,* having fun and making money together under a common cause.

EARN $500 to $1,000 PER MONTH

If your present job has a *frozen* income, there's a place for you in Network Marketing. A **PART TIME** home-based business is an excellent way to earn a *little* more money for those who enjoy their *regular* job.

Find a *product* in a Network Marketing company that you like, put as little as 10 to 12 hours a week (not three or four like many tell you), and you *could* bring home that extra $500 to $1,000 per month within a few months.

Doesn't seem like much? *Hey!* That's up to you. Set your own goals. Put in another several hours and DOUBLE that—maybe. It costs so very little to try.

It's simply amazing how the *amount you earn* doing anything is almost *directly related* to the amount of *effort* you put into it. If you'll notice, those who work the hardest and the smartest always seem to have the most. They're often not necessarily the smartest people either, are they?

MOST NETWORK MARKETING COMPANIES

I think the OLD way—alone—is tough to work and the reason why so many do not even *attempt* Network Marketing. The word *"marketing"* means *"selling"* something and many people don't want to, don't know *how,* or REFUSE to SELL! Certain personalities are just not conducive to selling *anything*.

I've found the KEY to take the **SELLING OUT,** and put the **TELLING IN!** Get my 10-page Info Packet. Remember, it's FREE. Learn HOW I am able to create a "warm market" of strangers, all calling YOU for information.

ONE good radio show could build an **entire downline** for you. And, remember, I do them FOR YOU and they are **FREE**! I conduct (fun)MEETINGS for you and they are **FREE**! I do phone interviews for and with you and they are **FREE**! I **DUPLICATE** with you and show you HOW I was able to make several MILLION dollars by networking. IF you are willing to work, and if I can help, contact me anytime.

"Money is a way of keeping COUNT on how well you're doing in business."

John D. Rockefeller

Chapter 7

SKYBIZ 2000 TESTIMONIALS

I've bragged about, mentioned, and told you about **SkyBiz 2000** throughout this book. WHY? Because it makes MORE MONEY for their distributors than ANY Network Marketing business in the world today! I MUST end my book on this company.

Stuart Purcell, a friend for many years who helped edit this book is the one who bought the round of drinks for "everybody in the bar," has NEVER made this much money before in his life.

Many people hesitate and/or refuse to say how MUCH money they're making for fear of their safety (among other reasons). Stuart never TOLD me how much money he was making, but if my calculations are correct, I'd say that Stuart is now at $42,000 a WEEK. He's been in **SkyBiz 2000** for only TEN MONTHS!

It's no fun to be poor but it is totally **devastating** to be rich and THEN become poor. It happened to me 15 years ago. I still had friends who would "sponsor" me to meals, plane trips, etc. They were rich. But I didn't want to be "kept" (so to speak) and since I couldn't "run" with the pack, I had to *leave* the pack. But, I made it again and I'm absolutely THRILLED; not smug, not arrogant, not bragging, THRILLED!

RESIDUAL INCOME is what you want. There is this one man in **SkyBiz 2000** whom I refer to as *The Alien*. After but EIGHT MONTHS in **SkyBiz** he and his family moved from Reno, Nevada to Australia. About six weeks ago his income was at about $90,000 a week. Then it grew to $128,000. PER WEEK! And he did NOTHING but let time pass. He has distributors UNDER him, 99% of whom he doesn't even KNOW, and when *they* make money, HE makes money. That's working SMART.

My friend Stuart lives in California. He had a successful financial consulting firm for the past 20 years. Previously he practiced as a CPA and a Certified Financial Planner. When he saw **SkyBiz 2000** and knew about computers and the fact that in 1992 there were NO web sites, but in 1999, the United States *alone* had 100 MILLION on the Internet, Stuart jumped at this opportunity to make some big money. He had no idea HOW big it would be.

NOW, as a financial professional who "has made his," his *mission* is to help others by reaching around the world to assist people to realize their dreams, IF they are willing to help themselves.

"***Give*** *a man a fish and feed him for a day.* ***Teach*** *a man to fish, and feed him* ***forever****."*

My dear, sweet, bright, caring friend, Stuart, has some things to share with you about **SkyBiz 2000.**

"First off, **SkyBiz 2000** is PROVEN! It is not mere

conversation, it is *documentation*! Massive incomes are already being made. In my opinion, **SkyBiz 2000** will set every record in the history of the world as to compensation paid. This isn't just Network Marketing, it is all business and commerce. Currently, **SkyBiz 2000 is paying out $1,500,000+ in commissions each week!**

"What is happening here has never happened in the history of the WORLD. I can't envision a like happening in my lifetime. If I was given a choice of being in ANY profession in the world, my choice would **INTERNET MARKETING.** ***I am where I want to be!***

"To fulfill my *mission*, I want every person to be successful with **SkyBiz 2000.** I will do whatever I can to personally assure this occurs.

"Boy, it's great to be out of poverty. YOU can do it, too. Your *group building phase* should take from 3 to 12 months. On a FUN FACTOR scale of from 1 to 10, **SkyBiz 2000** is a **15!** ENJOY your work. ENJOY your dreams. ENJOY making them a reality!"

RIGHT PRESCRIPTION FOR THE DOCTOR

Another friend I asked to tell her story in this book is Dr. Margaret Yates. Margaret had been an EMPLOYEE trading hours for dollars most of her life. She is a Ph.D. who, for 19 years, worked as a School Psychologist and as she stated, "*Networking was a foreign concept to me.*"

Stuart (Purcell) called her and told her about

SkyBiz 2000. *"I joined but just watched things happen for months.* I saw *Stuart raking in money, and on December 5, 1999 I began to focus on* ***SkyBiz 2000.*** *WHAT A PAYOFF!*

"In the last two weeks of January I earned the equivalent of ***ONE HALF MY ANNUAL INCOME*** *as a School Psychologist! The money kept streaming in and now far exceeds my monthly income with my Ph.D. The last week in January I earned $25,000! This next year I should earn at least $250,000.*

"How did I do it? A strong desire to improve the quality of my life and by using only moderate people skills. The payoff is more than just money. It is 'time freedom' and peace of mind.

"It is never having to do what you DON'T want to do FOR money, and never NOT doing what you want to do BECAUSE of money."

SLEEPLESS IN SEATTLE

Larry and Monica, a husband and wife team, have had tremendous success. I spoke with Monica earlier this evening and she shared some things with me. They had just returned from a skiing vacation.

"Pete, so many Network Marketers are AFRAID to get out of their 'comfort zone' with another Network Marketing company and move to SkyBiz. I do not WANT them to move, I want them to stay in what they are doing and work ***SkyBiz 2000*** *along WITH their present company. They can advertise on their* ***SkyBiz***

web site to sell whatever it is they are selling.

"We joined SkyBiz for a $100 membership to build a web site to promote ANOTHER company—one we were involved in at the time. One MLM we were with went out of business and we know what it feels like to go from $30,000 a month to NOTHING! I personally think it's WISE to get a second company as INSURANCE against the first one.

We "orbited" 200 times last WEEK in ***SkyBiz*** *while Larry and I were on that skiing jaunt to Canada. Am I excited? Who wouldn't be?"*

I asked husband Larry for a testimonial. He's working on it. While I'm waiting for his "words of wisdom" I want to tell you some of what I got from Stuart. . .

★*"For only $110 out-of-pocket cost, in 10 months of working SkyBiz, I'm looking forward to a year that I MIGHT make two million dollars; I mean* ***TWO MILLION DOLLARS!***

"Let me tell you about a friend. His name is Dr. Kenneth Long, pastor of Visionary Community Church in Phoenix. In eight months with ***SkyBiz*** *the church received $30,000."*

★ **DR. KENNETH LONG:** *"My heart is bubbling over with heartfelt gratitude. What a financial boost! Because of our good fortune I can find it easy to recommend* ***SkyBiz 2000*** *as a fund raiser for ANY faith* *organizations and charitable causes. In this **SkyBiz** program of cooperative free enterprise (versus competitive capitalism), it is possible for the people to earn great money and at the same time strengthen the charity/cause of their choice."*

★ **ON THE INTERNET:** 70,000+ people PER DAY are signing up.

★ **HOME-BASED BUSINESSES:** 25,000 per day.

★ **WEBSITES:** IBM Research says 100,000 a day, soon to be 125,000, 150,000, (in the words of Yul Brynner from The King and I) etc., etc., etc.

★ **SKYBIZ 2000:** President, Jim Brown says: "*This company is now the #2 website provider in the WORLD! There are over 300,000 in our company with 4,000 to 5,000 coming in each day. Any day now, we will be* **THE #1 WEBSITE PROVIDER IN THE WORLD!"**

★ **KEN BACKOFEN** (retired corporate executive in Hudson Valley NY): "*SkyBiz is the most powerful thing ever to come into existence. Nothing on this planet compares to **SkyBiz 2000."***

★ **DAVE ZARUCA** (Multi-millionaire friend in Ohio). Dave works with the Catholic and Baptist churches in the Toledo area.): **"SkyBiz 2000** is **THE ULTIMATE**

FUND RAISER!"

★ **JEFF BECKER:** Another **SkyBiz** friend, found just TWO individuals who "worked the business." These two built a group under Jeff and he is now in the 5-figure a week income. Oh, Jeff worked. He worked smart.

★ **MALCOLM WALLACE** (Canada): "*The **bottom 50%** of my team is right at $400 to $2,000 a week.*"

★ **COMPANY FACTS** (six-months report ending with the year 1999): Exactly 3.2% earned between $1,000 and $25,000 a week. 13 members earned more than $25,000 a week average.

★ Within three years there will be more than **THREE HUNDRED MILLION** MORE Internet users.

★ **STUART PURCELL**: "*Money is not the answer; money just gives you options. Because of **SkyBiz 2000** my life and lifestyle have changed. Three weeks ago I had Lasik laser eyesight correction; I threw away my glasses. I bought that bar a round of drinks. I made a major donation to my church. For my birthday I'm buying that new luxury sports car I always wanted.*"

★ **LARRY EDWARDS**: *Finally, the fax came in from Larry and his story is a good one.* Larry was a career construction engineer for 20 years. He worked the typical 40-hour week x 50 weeks that amounted to right at 2,000 hours a year. If he worked for FORTY years that would be 80,000 of these "man hours."

Years ago, Larry attended a Networking Seminar and learned that if he could make a few referrals to a few friends, and if they duplicated *his* efforts, he could, theoretically, be the beneficiary of these 80,000 man hours it would take him FORTY YEARS to accumulate, in only 18 months.

He has been in networking for the last few years and had some financial success, "*But not until I paid my $100 and got in this fabulous web site program, did I realize the potential of networking.*

*"Forty-four weeks ago we started with **SkyBiz 2000.** From the personal referrals I got from enrolling **20** friends, I now have 230,000 customer/members in over 75 countries. What a worldwide opportunity for me, my family, and my friends.*

"*I am no rocket scientist nor am I a super salesman. My wife and I worked as a team and we built a comfortable income. I rejected this program 5 times before I admitted, reluctantly, that the Internet and the computer and telephones were ALL that I needed to make a lot of money.*

*"From the original seven friends, it grew to 1,000 members in 30 days. Then the group doubled and redoubled month after month. After but 44 weeks of my life working **SkyBiz 2000**, 16 people in my group are earning a SEVEN DIGIT ANNUAL INCOME! And THEIR income will grow and maybe double and*

double again in time.

"We're making some money! All of this we built from our home with the help of our family computer and the telephone. And the good part about having a home-based business, I ESPECIALLY LOVE THE COMMUTE!"

MONICA ADDS HER NO-BRAINER

This is how AMAZING this program is and how it COULD work for you. Sponsor only TWO people, all within a month and let it go!

If those two EACH sponsored two in the next month, that = 6 (the original two YOU sponsored and the 2 each THEY sponsored).

If those 4 do likewise and if the THEORETICAL formula continues (some will sponsor more and some will *die on the vine*), it's conceivable that, in **SkyBiz 2000,** by the end of but a single year you will have **8000** in your downline.

Now, the **SkyBiz 2000** ORBIT PLAN awards you in *sets* of 50. This means you orbit 160 times and an orbit pays between $400 to $600. What *this* means is somewhere between $64,000 and $96,000 is what you would have earned!

If these SAME PEOPLE do nothing more than RENEW THEIR MEMBERSHIP, it means that you would receive the same income year, after year, after year. Sounds unbelievable? It did to us. But, WE TRIED IT.

I sponsored 20 of my friends. From those 20 members, within a 41-week window, 200,000 have enrolled in our world-wide window. I am NOW "orbiting" more than **ONE TIME PER HOUR!**

AWESOME? **YES**! UNBELIEVABLE? **NO!**

Anyone Can Do It!

A FINANCIAL QUIZ
(Circle your answer)

1. Do you have a job? Yes No

2. Do you LIKE that job? Yes No

3. Are you earning what you're worth? Yes No

4. Are you in the mood to make some SERIOUS income? Yes No

5. Would you LIKE to make a lot of money? Yes No

6. Would you like to be RICH? Yes No

7. Are you willing to do whatever it takes to be rich? Yes No

8. Do you have a computer? Yes No

9. Are you aware that the Internet is the fastest growing industry in the world? Yes No

10. Do you believe the Internet is here to stay? Yes No

11. Do you think there is SERIOUS MONEY that can be made on the Internet? Yes No

12. Do you know anyone making money on the Internet? Yes No

13. Are YOU presently earning money on the Internet? Yes No

14. Would you take a few minutes and look at the e.mail address on the last page (sticker) and look up SkyBiz 2000? Yes No

15. If you e-mail me, I'll e-mail you back. Is that okay with you? Yes No

A PERFECT SCORE is if you answered YES to 4,5, 6, 7, 14 and 15.

AUTHOR'S CLOSING COMMENTS

I NEVER advocate setting *unrealistic* goals, but with dozens and dozens in **SkyBiz 2000** reaching for and passing a MILLION dollars and many, MANY more at a HALF million dollars a year within ONE year of being in the business, THAT is awesome! Breath-taking and unbelievable. *Really!*

They say that the Internet doubles every 100 days. Now, think of HOW MANY PEOPLE you know who OWN a computer. Contact them NOW! Sit behind your computer at home and have a telephone close by. Call and e-mail. E-mail and call. Contact EVERY-ONE you know or can think of.

With four or five people on each side, you are in business. Friends, TOO MANY are successful with **SkyBiz 2000** for *you* NOT to try. It costs 10% more than a hundred bucks, for goodness sakes, and you are in business for yourself for ONE year. NO over-head. NO boss. NO limit on what you can earn. And, a CHANCE to be rich.

It might seem that I'm PUSHING you toward **SkyBiz 2000—AND I AM!!!** If you're making enough money (whatever THAT amount is) in your present job and want to stay, by all means stay. But at least LOOK into **SkyBiz 2000** and determine if you'd like to TRY it, maybe part-time.

If you ARE interested in making money over the Internet, becoming an **INTERNET MILLIONAIRE**, please LOOK at **SkyBiz 2000** as a home-based business. You would LIKE to be rich, wouldn't you? Maybe you didn't know how. **NOW, you do!**

Look for a sticker on the last page of the book and call that person. They will tell you all that you need to know. You won't be "pushed," only informed. They will only give you an Internet Code, and it tells you, step-by-step, what you have to do. If you have any questions, ask them for answers. It's simple. You can join in minutes using your credit card and begin work IMMEDIATELY.

Then, whoever **you** call and interest in joining from that moment on is UNDER YOU. And whoever they call and interest is under them *and* under you. And whoever *they* call counts for all the above and on, and on, and ON! It's LEGAL, it's SMART, it is NOT a PYRAMID.

This IS the one where you might get TWO people (one on each side or LEG), and "*sail away on that yacht to Tahiti.*" Of course, if you get TWO on each side or THREE or FIVE, your chances for success multiply enormously. LOOK at that simple example (NO-BRAINER) and se how easy it CAN be.

AND, if you don't know anyone, if you have NO friends, NO relatives and NO neighbors, if you have total AMNESIA, punch in MY e-mail at the end of this book and I'll tell you how I can bring a "warm market" to you though this book.

I WANT you to be rich and successful. And then, do GOOD with those riches. It truly is YOURS FOR THE TAKING if you want to take that chance. Donald

Trump, in an interview on the David Letterman show about two years ago, said "*If I went broke tomorrow, I'd go into some form of Network Marketing.*"

The industry of Network Marketing truly IS fascinating; it has made MORE millionaires in the past decade than *any* business—even counting the enormous amount of money movie stars, entertainers, and athletes are getting paid, and this includes winners of the state lotteries.

If you approach Networking Marketing like a *game*, it makes it fun and keeps you interested. So WHAT if you lose a time or two? Keep playing the game. If you don't like game playing, go ahead and make it work. Again, it's not how many times you get *knocked down*, it's how many times you get back UP!

Good luck and God bless.

Pete Billac

ABOUT THE AUTHOR

PETE BILLAC is one of the most sought-after speakers in the United States. He has written 49 full-length books, hundreds of short stories and he makes his audiences laugh—hard. His worldwide best seller, HOW NOT TO BE LONELY, sold over four million copies.

Pete is a maverick; he writes what pleases him. His topics range from adventure to war, the Mafia, famous people, to romance, love, health, motivation, and how to make money!

He gives seminars almost monthly for Fortune 500 companies on marketing, and at universities across America. He offers his services free to grammar and high schools where he speaks about reading and writing, and conducts fun lectures on cruise ships.

Pete is currently traveling the world telling how to be successful with home based businesses. *"This book, INTERNET MILLIONAIRE, tells people how to become rich. Making money is great—and easy, too, if you believe in yourself and work smart. God wants you to be prosperous, and to help others along the way."*

Perhaps you've seen Pete on Donahue, Sally Jessy Raphael, Good Morning America, Laff Stop and other national televison shows. He mixes common sense and knowledge with laughter. He charms his audiences, and breathes life into every topic.

"Pete is an expert at restoring self-confidence and self-esteem in others . . ."

Phil Donahue
National Television Talk Show Host

BECOME AN Internet Millionaire

is available through:

Swan Publishing
126 Live Oak
Alvin, TX 77511

(281) 388-2547
Fax (281) 585-3738

or e-mail: swanbooks@ghg.net
Visit our web site at:
http:\\www.swan-pub.com

For more information on SkyBiz 2000, call:

After reading this book, please pass it on to a friend or relative. It could change their lives for the better—FOREVER.